Castle Campb

Stewart Cruden

HISTORIC SCOTLAND

'OURE souverane Lord of his Riale autorite at the desire and Supplicacioun of his cousing and traist consalor Coline erle of Ergile, lord campbele and lorne his chancellare has chengeit the name of the castelle and place quhilk wes callit the gloume pertenying to his said cousing And in his present pliament [parliament] maks mutacioun and chenging of the said Name And ordinis the samyn castell to be callit in tyme to cum Campbele.'

(Act of Parliament, 1489-90)

A Guided Tour

This tour guides the visitor around the castle, beginning at the entrance gateway on the north side and ending at 'John Knox's Pulpit' on the south.

Castle Campbell was designed to serve three main purposes: to provide adequate defence; to look imposing as a conspicuous statement of its lord's wealth and power; and to provide the accommodation required by the extensive household of a member of the senior nobility. The level of importance of these needs changed at various times, though in general it is probably true to say that as time went on comfort and architectural elegance tended to overtake defensibility.

The accommodation required was extensive. There had to be not only a residence for the lord and his immediate family, but also lodgings for his extended household, from high-ranking members to 'menials'. He also had to provide hospitality to guests, including royalty and other noblemen with their large travelling entourages.

The owner's private residence was originally the self-contained and independently secure tower house [2]. Later owners, however, may have preferred to occupy the hall and chamber range [3], with further accommodation for senior members of their household and important guests in the adjacent east range [4]. In addition to being more spacious, the hall and chamber range had the advantage of overlooking the terraced gardens [5] on the south-facing slopes of the hill above Dollar.

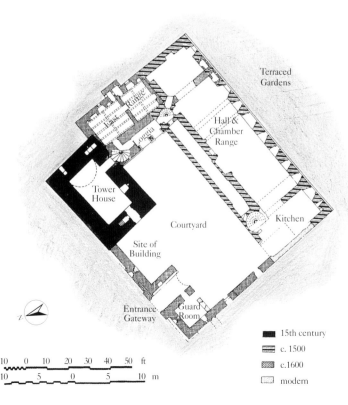

Terraced Gardens

East Range

Loggia

Hall & Chamber Range

Tower House

Courtyard

Kitchen

Site of Building

Entrance Gateway

Guard Room

10 0 10 20 30 40 50 ft
10 5 0 5 10 m

■ 15th century
▤ c. 1500
▨ c.1600
▢ modern

3

1 Entrance Gateway and Guardroom

An adequate defence was achieved by the construction of a thick main **courtyard wall** enclosing all the main buildings. In the earliest buildings, windows towards the outside world were few, particularly along the more vulnerable north side, where the tower house only had windows on the top floor.

Emphasising the appearance of strength, two wide-mouthed gunholes flank the later sixteenth-century **entrance gateway** through the courtyard wall. The doors were strengthened on the inside by timber draw-bars, the deep slot for which can be seen within the passage. Also within the passage are a stone bench and a locker. The **guardroom**, or porter's lodge (now the steward's office), was originally reached off the west side of the passage.

All of this provided an essentially passive form of defence, sufficient to repel a lightly-armed raid, but certainly not enough to withstand a siege supported by artillery. In an age when family feuds often led to armed hostility, and a nobleman's house had to serve as a repository for his valuables, such defences were advisable, though they need not be oppressive.

Gunhole

Entrance to Guardroom
(blocked)

Gunhole

Castle Campbell from the north-west, and (inset) the entrance gateway.

2 The Tower House

The tower house is characteristic of the late fifteenth century, being of simple oblong plan, with massively thick walls pierced by few windows, and rising to a slightly overhanging parapet 18 m above the ground. There are four main floors, each with a single room, and a garret in the roof space. The ground, first and top floors are covered by stone barrel vaults.

As first built, the tower house had **two entrances**. That into the west face of the ground floor was perhaps primarily a service doorway, while the main entrance was on the south side of the first floor. Because of the irregularities of the rock on which the tower house was built, the service doorway was originally well above the external ground level. It opened into a short passage through the wall, from the left side of which a straight flight of stairs led up to the first floor. The passage opened into a vaulted **storage cellar** with slit windows in its south wall, one of which was later enlarged to form a doorway opening onto the spiral stair added on this side of the tower house in about 1600.

The upper entrance gave access through a small lobby into the hall. This doorway was originally reached by an outside stair, probably of timber, which was removed when the new stair was built around 1600 (see the reconstruction drawing on p.21). To the right of the entrance lobby is a wall-closet which gave access to a **pit-prison** beneath, formed in the wall thickness. The lord was responsible for local law enforcement, and a secure place of confinement was needed for those awaiting judgement.

The first-floor hall looking towards the fireplace. The fine buffet recess is on the left.

The **first-floor hall** was the principal 'reception' room of the tower house. The fireplace, with plain sides and a segmental-arched head below a chamfered cornice, occupies much of the east wall. High in the wall beside it a small window lights this end of the room, and there

is a similar window in the opposite wall. The main window at this level was in the south wall, overlooking the courtyard, and, like many of the windows of the tower house, has been enlarged at some stage. In the north wall are the remains of an ogee-arched buffet recess; ostentatious display was an essential way of expressing status, and the lord's best plate would have been on show here during mealtimes.

The (now headless) 'winged beast' water-spout at the wall-head.

The upper floors and wall-head were originally reached by a narrow spiral stair within the wall thickness at the south-west corner of the tower house. This went out of use in about 1600 when the new stair was built and the east range remodelled. The upper parts of the old stairwell were converted into wall-closets.

The **second-floor room** was a private chamber, perhaps the outer room of a two-room lodging for the lord, the inner chamber being on the floor above. This room is not vaulted, but has a timber floor carried on

The tower house from the south-west.

corbels (projecting stones) which, for no obvious reason, are more widely spaced in the eastern half of the room. The fireplace is in the north wall, and within its right side is a small aumbry (cupboard) probably for keeping salt dry. In the wall to the right of the fireplace is an L-shaped latrine closet, with a seat, a waste chute and a recess for an oil lamp. There is another closet within what was the stairwell, in the corner of the room diagonally opposite the latrine. All the windows on this floor have been modified, and the south window has been greatly enlarged to take advantage of the stunning view.

The **third-floor room** was perhaps originally the lord's inner (bed) chamber. The present entrance, built about 1600 when the east range was remodelled, passed through what used to be a wall-closet. The stone vault over the room was also added in 1600. Like those over the ground floor of the east range, it has cross-ribs, with a ridge-rib running from end to end. The highlight of the vault is a pair of grotesque 'green man' masks, from the mouths of which lights would have been suspended. The insertion of the vault necessitated blocking the south window, and cutting a smaller one through the north wall. The window in the west wall has been enlarged. The fireplace in the east wall has moulded capitals, and in the north-east corner is a latrine closet.

The **roof** was destroyed when the castle fell into ruin; the present roof was built after the castle was taken into State care in 1948. Running around it is a wall-walk, set behind a parapet which slightly overhangs the tower-house walls and is carried on a single projecting corbel course. At the angles of the walk are projecting roundels. The wall-walk and roundels were drained by water-spouts carved as grotesque beasts. One winged beast, now unfortunately headless, survives on the north-west roundel, and stumps of four others can be seen along the west side.

A cut-open reconstruction of the tower house as it might have looked about 1600 (David Simon).

The pair of grotesque 'green man' masks on the third-floor room ceiling.

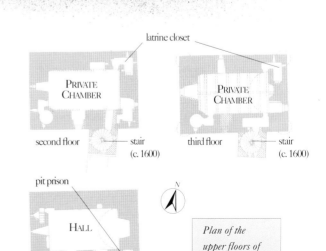

Plan of the upper floors of the tower house (the ground-floor plan is on p.3).

7

3 The Hall and Chamber Range

The range along the south side of the courtyard, now roofless and partly ruined, provided space for a much grander reception room than could be accommodated within the tower house (see the reconstruction drawing on p.24). The two levels of chambers at its east end may have superseded those provided for the earl in the tower house, though they have undergone a number of changes during their period of use.

Set slightly below the courtyard level, the ground floor contains **five cellars**, all stone-vaulted. Each is lit by a narrow slit window and has stone benching along the side walls. The cellars were entered from a corridor (now open to the elements). A vaulted pend (passage) at the west end of the range connected the courtyard with the gardens.

The principal rooms at first-floor level were reached from the courtyard by **two projecting stair turrets**. The principal entrance was by the west stair, which gave access to the lower end of the hall and to the kitchen; it is topped by an octagonal caphouse. The doorway into the main stair has three shields on the lintel, and there was an armorial panel near the top of the turret; all would have been brightly painted. The other stair, later absorbed within the east range, opened onto the dais (upper end) of the hall and the chambers, and would have been for private use. The two stair turrets were linked by an upper corridor, later much altered, above another which ran between the cellars.

In its overall design, and in the details of the main stair turret, this range bears a striking resemblance to the royal lodging, known as the King's Old Building, built for James IV at Stirling Castle in the 1490s. This reminds us that the earl moved in royal circles and must have been much influenced by the buildings he saw at the king's residences.

The **first floor of the range** was planned to provide a lodging of hall and chambers, together with a kitchen. The main room, at the centre of the range, was the **hall**. This has a fine row of windows overlooking the gardens to the south. A great fireplace in the north wall heated the body of the room, and there may have been a smaller one at the east end for the dais. The hall itself probably rose up through the equivalent of two storeys into an open-timber roof, but there were two storeys of rooms at each end. Those on the west were probably a **kitchen** and upper chamber, while those on the east may have provided **two storeys of chambers** for the lord. At a later stage the hall was reduced in size, when additional chambers were inserted at the east end. At the same time some of the windows were enlarged, and latrine closets for the chambers were carved out of the south wall.

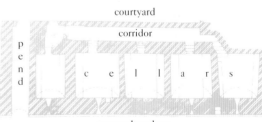

Plan of the hall and chamber range at basement level (the first-floor plan is on p.3).

*Main picture: The hall and chamber range from the terrace gardens;
(inset left) the range from the tower-house roof, and (inset right) the west stair
turret from the entrance gateway.*

The stair turret added to the tower house c. 1600.

4 The East Range

In its present form the east range dates from about 1600, but it is likely to incorporate earlier buildings. What remains of its facade towards the courtyard shows that it was a very sophisticated piece of design, constructed of fine ashlar with narrow joints. Each storey was defined by a moulded string-course, and has handsomely proportioned windows. There were **stair turrets** at each end of the courtyard facade: that to the south was the remodelled private stair of the hall and chamber range, while that to the north gave improved access into the various floors of the tower house as well as interlinking the floors of the east range.

Between the two stairs there was a corridor on each floor. That on the ground floor took the form of a **loggia**, or open arcade, formed of two segmental arches carried on a pier of clustered shafts. Such arcades were not common in wet and windy Scotland, but there are traces of examples at the castles of St Andrews and Huntly, and they seem to have been regarded as a feature of great elegance.

The **ground floor** contains two chambers covered by ribbed vaults similar to that inserted in the top storey of the tower house. The upper floors now contain the steward's flat and are not open to visitors.

The east range and part of the hall and chamber range from the tower-house roof.

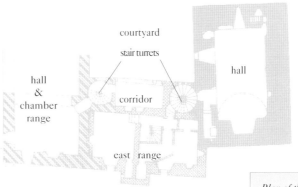

courtyard
stair turrets
hall
hall & chamber range
corridor
east range

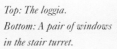

Top: The loggia.
Bottom: A pair of windows in the stair turret.

Plan of the east range at first-floor level (the ground-floor plan is on p.3).

5 The Gardens and 'John Knox's Pulpit'

To the south of the castle buildings, and reached via the pend through the hall and chamber range, are the **terraced gardens**. These were an important adjunct to the castle, intended for the exclusive use of the lord, his family and guests. Here they would have strolled and sat, taking in the stunning panorama and conversing privately, while breathing in the sweet smell of the flowers and herbs. The colourful spectacle was also intended to be enjoyed by them from the comfort of their halls and chambers. Though the gardens have never been archaeologically investigated, we can imagine them formally laid out, with raised flower beds and gravelled walks (see the reconstruction drawing on p.21).

To complement the pleasure garden there would have been a **kitchen garden**, providing vegetables, herbs and fruits for the lord's table. This may have been situated to the west of the castle and reached through the doorway on the west side of the courtyard.

A rocky knoll at the top of Kemp's Score, a fissure in the rock at the south-west corner of the terraced garden, has come to be known as **'John Knox's Pulpit'**. Local tradition says that during his stay at the castle in about 1556 the fiery Protestant preached from here to a large congregation but there is no foundation for this (see p.25). The ruined archway on the knoll is likely to have been a postern, or back gate, in the castle's outer defences, though the descent into the glen from here must always have been extremely hazardous.

Kemp's Score itself is said to have been cut by the giant robber, Kemp, who was supposedly caught and killed here after stealing the king's dinner from Dunfermline Castle. This and other place-names associated with Castle Campbell, including especially the Burns of Care and Sorrow, are suitably romantic and intriguing, complementing perfectly the dramatically-sited ruined castle.

The terraced gardens and south panorama from the tower-house roof. 'John Knox's' pulpit' is on the far right.

13

The Story of Castle Campbell

The story of Castle Campbell is inextricably linked
with the history of the Campbells themselves, who were
seldom far from the major political and religious events
of the fifteenth, sixteenth and seventeenth centuries.

*A winter scene at Castle Campbell. The arms depicted
are those of the Campbell Earls of Argyll.*

The Place of Gloom

The date the site was first fortified is unknown. However, the grassy mound on which the tower house stands (see the photograph on p.2) has a partly artificial appearance suggestive of a motte, or castle mound, of the type first introduced into Scotland by Anglo-Norman and Flemish settlers in the twelfth century. There is also a hint of a silted-up ditch across the promontory, which could have provided a defensive barrier for the earlier castle against attack from the vulnerable landward side.

The earliest known reference to the castle is a papal bull of 1466 which ordered that the Church was to punish Walter Stewart of Lorne for his destruction of 'a certain manor with a tower of the place of Glowm situated in the territory of Dollar'. (The place-name Gloom may be derived from the Gaelic 'Glom', meaning chasm, an apt description of the spectacular Dollar Glen below the castle). A charter dated 9 April in the previous year had testified that the lands were then already held by the Stewarts of Innermeath and Lorne from the Bishop of Dunkeld, which suggests that Stewart must have fallen out badly with his feudal superior for some reason.

It is usually said that the tower house we now see was built after the fire of 1466. However, since there are marks of burning and signs of subsequent rebuilding within the tower, it is possible it had been first built in the mid 1400s. The other buildings of the manor at that time were probably at least partly of timber.

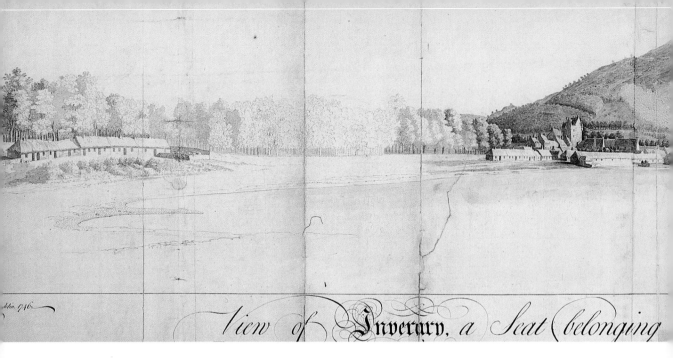

View of Inverary, a Seat (belonging

Castle Campbell

The estates of what was to become Castle Campbell were acquired by the Campbell family in the second half of the fifteenth century. At that time, the lands of the Stewarts of Lorne came to be divided among three heiresses, and it was by their marriages that the lands passed to the Campbells, a Highland family with strong aspirations to expand into the Lowlands. Colin, the second Lord Campbell and first Earl of Argyll, who eventually acquired the lion's share of these holdings, married Elizabeth Stewart in about 1465. He was a man high in royal favour, who was to enjoy many of the great offices of state. He was also a favoured ambassador, and as early as 1448 had been sent to France to renew the 'auld alliance' with that country.

A secure but impressive seat at the heart of the kingdom, within easy reach of the main centres of the king's court, was a necessity for this Highland nobleman. The acquisition of Gloom provided him with an ideal location. Argyll owed much to the patronage of James III, but while he was in England in 1488, his royal master was murdered after the Battle of Sauchieburn, near Stirling. Fortunately for Argyll, he continued to enjoy royal favour, and it was James IV who by act of parliament in 1489-90 approved the change of name of Argyll's Lowland seat from the mysterious Castle Gloom to the more prosaic Castle Campbell.

Clan Campbell

The Campbells (from the Gaelic *Na Caimbeulach*, 'men of the twisted mouths') became the most powerful clan in the western Highlands during the later Middle Ages. Their origins are obscure, but they had links with the ancient Britons of Strathclyde, and even claimed that they could trace their roots back to the legendary King Arthur.

The clan comprised several leading families, among them Argyll, Breadalbane and Cawdor, and a number of minor ones. Pre-eminent among them was the house of Argyll.

The clan's rise to power began during the Wars of Independence in the early fourteenth century when they allied themselves with Robert Bruce against the Comyns and Macdougalls, hitherto masters in the western Highlands. As a result, the monarchy steadily built up the power of the Campbells in the problematic west. As royal lieutenants they were instrumental in the long and turbulent dismemberment of the MacDonald empire.

The commitment of the Campbell chiefs to Presbyterianism in the seventeenth century quickly unravelled these close ties with the Stuart dynasty. The execution of the first Marquis in 1661 for supporting Cromwell was followed by that of his son in 1685 for his part in the rebellion against James VII. James's flight into exile in 1688 saw the house of Argyll restored and a dukedom conferred. Now more than ever the Campbell clan became a focus of resentment among the largely Catholic and Episcopalian clans, but the failure of the last Jacobite rising in 1746 resulted in the Campbells becoming undisputed leaders of the western Highlands.

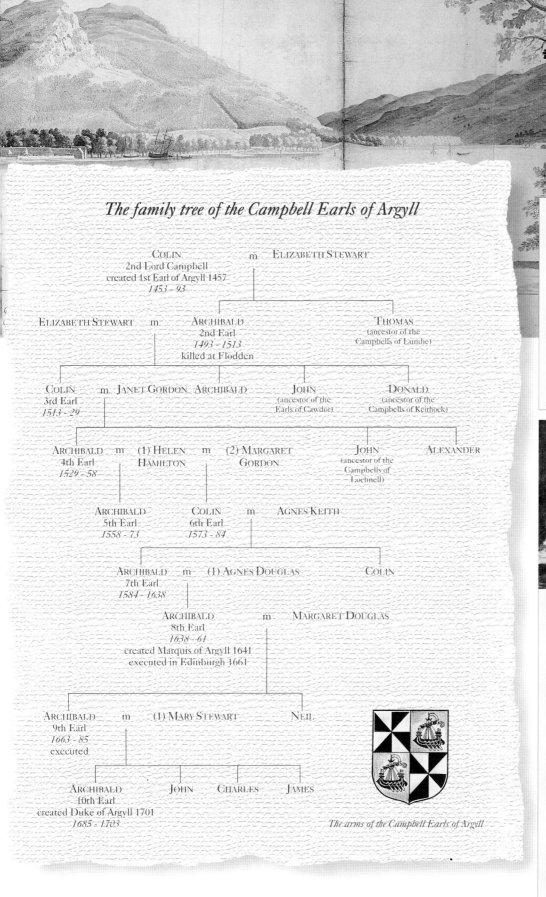

The family tree of the Campbell Earls of Argyll

COLIN
2nd Lord Campbell
created 1st Earl of Argyll 1457
1453 - 93
    m   ELIZABETH STEWART

ELIZABETH STEWART   m   ARCHIBALD
2nd Earl
1493 - 1513
killed at Flodden

THOMAS
(ancestor of the
Campbells of Lundie)

COLIN
3rd Earl
1513 - 29
   m   JANET GORDON   ARCHIBALD

JOHN
(ancestor of the
Earls of Cawdor)

DONALD
(ancestor of the
Campbells of Keithock)

ARCHIBALD
4th Earl
1529 - 58
  m   (1) HELEN
HAMILTON
  m   (2) MARGARET
GORDON

JOHN
(ancestor of the
Campbells of
Lochnell)

ALEXANDER

ARCHIBALD
5th Earl
1558 - 73

COLIN
6th Earl
1573 - 84
  m   AGNES KEITH

ARCHIBALD
7th Earl
1584 - 1638
  m   (1) AGNES DOUGLAS

COLIN

ARCHIBALD
8th Earl
1638 - 61
created Marquis of Argyll 1641
executed in Edinburgh 1661
  m   MARGARET DOUGLAS

ARCHIBALD
9th Earl
1663 - 85
executed
  m   (1) MARY STEWART

NEIL

ARCHIBALD
10th Earl
created Duke of Argyll 1701
1685 - 1703

JOHN   CHARLES   JAMES

The arms of the Campbell Earls of Argyll

Inveraray and Loch Fyne, Argyllshire, by Paul Sandby (1746). Shortly after this scene was painted, the medieval tower-house castle of the Earls of Argyll (depicted centre left) was demolished and replaced by the present Inveraray Castle. (Courtesy of the National Galleries of Scotland.)

Archibald Campbell, eighth Earl and first Marquis of Argyll (1607-61). (Courtesy of His Grace the Duke of Argyll.) This picture is known as the 'Castle Campbell' portrait. The original painting, found in a cottage near Dollar in 1867, was destroyed in a fire at Inveraray Castle in 1877. Fortunately, the portrait had earlier been photographed, perhaps by D.O. Hill, a pioneer in the new art, who died in 1870.

Daily Life at the Castle

Castle Campbell would have been staffed at all times. When the Argyll family were away, this would have been a skeleton staff, sufficient to sort out the chaos left by the departing company and to keep the place secure and 'ticking over' until their return. But with the arrival of the lord and his considerable household - perhaps numbering 50 or more people - the whole complex would burst into life. During the earl's stay, the days would have been spent attending the king or parliament, dealing with estate matters in the castle, or sporting in the surrounding hills and forests. Many of the evenings would have been occasions for feasting and making merry.

To appreciate the daily life of the household in what might now appear a cold and inhospitable place, one must attempt to visualise the contemporary scene in all its detail and colour and to picture the hangings and furnishings which once enlivened the empty and lifeless rooms.

Most of the interior and exterior stonework would have been plastered or rendered over, with many of the carved and moulded details picked out in colour. Much of the impression of richness which the rooms once conveyed would have been created by lavish upholstery. In the earlier years of the castle's history, there would have been relatively little furniture in the rooms, for almost everything had to be capable of being packed into a baggage train and sent on to the lord's next 'port-of-call' - even his great bed with its canopy supported by four carved posts. By the end of the castle's history in the mid seventeenth century, however, there would probably have been more to be seen within the rooms.

The hall (both that in the tower house and the later one in the south range) had a great fireplace as its principal focus, for the hearth was the most potent symbol of hospitality. At one end of the hall would probably have been a slightly raised dais, where the 'hie buird' (high table) was set, probably with a cloth of estate embroidered with the Campbell arms hanging behind it to symbolise the high status of the castle's lord. Along the side walls other tables could be set if large numbers were to be fed. In the castle's earlier years these tables would have been boards supported on trestles, which could be removed when not needed. The boards would have been covered 'with cloth of costly green' similar to the green baize covering a modern snooker table. There would have been only one chair in the earlier days, reserved for the lord himself, or for

his principal guest if he was of higher status - hence the dignity of the name 'chairman' and the formal invitation to 'take the chair'. Others would have sat on benches or stools.

Table vessels were of wood, pewter or pottery, with silver reserved for use by the most important people and for display on the buffet. On the walls may have hung tapestries or embroideries adorned with woodland scenes or depictions of classical stories. The finest hangings were imported from the Continent. A boy with a pitcher of water would have been in attendance for those who wished to rinse their hands before and after eating, since much of the food was eaten by hand. The floor may have been strewn with grasses and herbs, which provided a pleasant aroma and were easily replaced. Later in the castle's history, woven mats made their appearance.

The main items of furniture in the bed chambers were the beds, which in the principal chambers would have had fine hangings. There may also have been truckle beds below the main beds for the use of servants (though most servants would have made do with straw-filled palliasses placed in whatever corner of the house they were able to make their own). The chambers would also have contained chests in which clothes, bedding and valuables could be safely stored, and perhaps a table.

AN INVENTORY OF 1595

The following is a selection of the items recorded in an inventory of the effects made in 1595, describing the furnishings then in the castle. A translation is also given.

in ye wardrup ane bordclauth for ye hie buird wowin upone ye thrade
in the wardrobe a woven tablecloth for the high table

thrie faldane cheir coverit wid leddir
three folding chairs covered with leather

yet tymber of ane grit standard bed
timber of a large [probably four-poster] bed

ane tapestrie of arras work
a tapestry made in Arras

sevin piece of grein tapestrie bandit wit rasor work
seven pieces of tapestry bound with smooth cloth of gold

in my lordis uttir chalmer four peice of hingard tapestrie, ane faldane comptar buird wit tua lang furmes
in my lord's outer chamber four pieces of hanging tapestry, a folding table with two long forms. [In an earlier age, table tops were squared for the reckoning or counting of money: hence counter or compter board.]

ane fyne cramoisie velvett mess clayth brouderit wit gold
a fine crimson Mass cloth embroidered with gold

tua auld ruiffes of beddis of red worsett
two old bed canopies [roofs] of red worsted

Castle Campbell as it might have looked about 1500. Archibald Campbell, fourth Earl of Argyll, and his retinue are pictured arriving at the castle for a short stay (David Simon).

Castles of the Campbells

The earliest recorded home of the Campbells of Argyll is Innis Chonnell, a thirteenth-century castle in Loch Awe; the family were then known as the Campbells of Lochawe. Innis Chonnell evidently served as their principal residence, though there were others, including Castle Sween, the oldest standing castle in Scotland, which Argyll acquired in 1481, and the forbidding Carrick Castle beside Loch Goil. In about 1450, the family moved their chief seat from Innis Chonnell to a new tower-house castle at Inveraray, beside Loch Fyne. This was demolished and replaced by the present building shortly after the '45 Jacobite rising came to a bloody end at Culloden.

The Campbells of Breadalbane (originally known as the Campbells of Glenorchy) had their chief residence at Kilchurn Castle, at the north end of Loch Awe, not far from Innis Chonnell. This formidable stronghold, begun in the mid fifteenth century by Colin Campbell, first Lord of Glenorchy and the first Earl of Argyll's uncle, matches the family's ambitions, which culminated in 1681 in their chief's elevation to the Earldom of Breadalbane. Barcaldine Castle, in Benderloch, built in the early seventeenth century, was also a residence of this cadet branch of the clan. Numerous other towers were built or acquired by the burgeoning Campbell kindred throughout the sixteenth and seventeenth centuries, and others like Carnasserie, in Kilmartin Glen, were built in open acknowledgement of Clan Campbell's superiority.

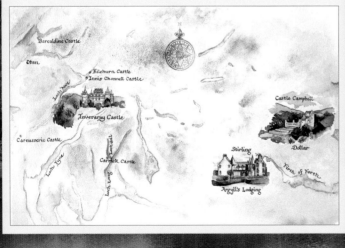

Kilchurn Castle, Loch Awe, the chief seat of the Campbells of Breadalbane.

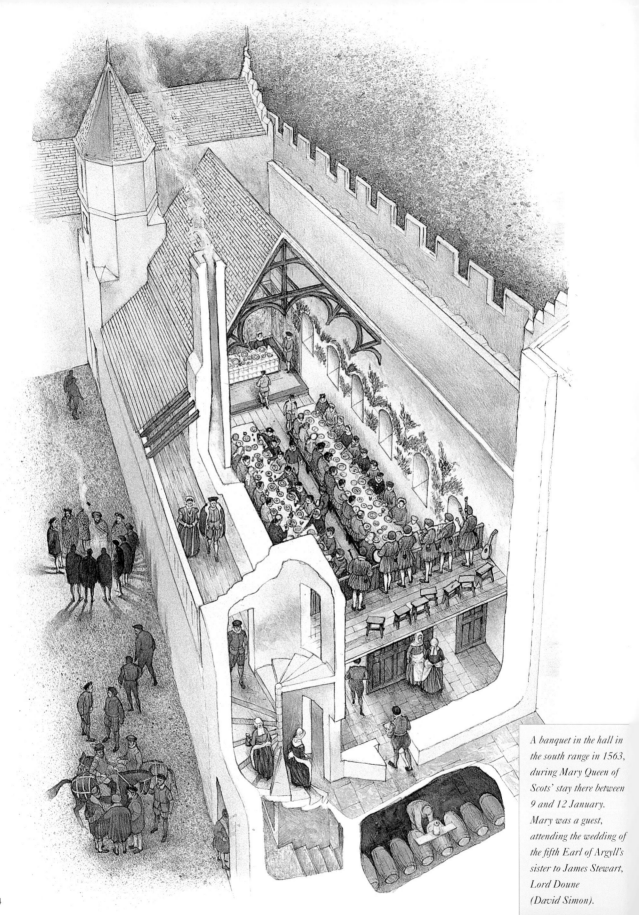

A banquet in the hall in the south range in 1563, during Mary Queen of Scots' stay there between 9 and 12 January. Mary was a guest, attending the wedding of the fifth Earl of Argyll's sister to James Stewart, Lord Doune (David Simon).

Important Visitors to the Castle

JOHN KNOX

For several decades little is known about Castle Campbell, but an important visit must be recorded in the time of Archibald, the fourth Earl. Archibald had distinguished himself as a military leader against the English at the Battle of Pinkie, near Musselburgh, in 1547 and subsequently at the long siege of Haddington. Archibald's religious sympathies were increasingly with the Protestant cause, and he was perhaps the first of the great noblemen to embrace the idea of Reformation with enthusiasm.

And so it was that during his time, probably in 1556 (four years before the Parliament of 1560 which marked the turning-point of the Scottish Reformation), that Castle Campbell received an important visitor - John Knox. This fiery advocate of Protestantism had encountered problems soon after beginning his preaching career in St Andrews in 1547, but following his return from exile in 1554, he gained strong support from Archibald Lord Lorne, Argyll's son and heir. According to Knox's own account, he 'passed to the old Erle of Ergyle, who was then in the Castell of Campbell, where he tawght certain dayis'.

According to tradition, Knox preached to a large congregation from the rocky knoll at the south-west corner of the castle grounds, known as 'John Knox's Pulpit' (see p.12). The small size of the knoll and the steep drops around it would have made it quite unsuitable for large gatherings, and in all probability the scene of Knox's teaching was within the hall in the south range. Following his stay, Knox left Scotland for France and Geneva.

John Knox, depicted on a stained-glass window in St Giles, Edinburgh.

MARY QUEEN OF SCOTS

Seven years after Knox's visit, the castle housed an even more illustrious visitor, Mary Queen of Scots.

Mary stayed at the castle from 9 to 12 January 1563. She had come to attend the wedding of the fifth Earl's sister, Margaret, to James Stewart, Lord Doune. The festivities included banquets and masques; one of these involved guests dressing up as shepherds and playing lutes. Two years later, however, Argyll had thrown in his lot with those who were in rebellion against the queen. In September of that year, Mary and Darnley, her second husband whom she had newly wed, passed close to Dollar Glen during their campaign against the rebels - the so-called 'Chaseabout Raid' - and received the surrender of the castle.

A variety of charters issued from the castle around this time cast an interesting light on the relationship between the earl and those who lived on his estates around the castle. As well as their feudal obligations of military service, they apparently had to keep the castle supplied with bread, meal, coal, ale and wine.

A Covenanting Stronghold

Given the continuing support of the Earls of Argyll for the Protestant cause, it was inevitable that their castle would be drawn into the political and religious events that dominated Scottish life in the seventeenth century. Archibald, the eighth Earl, who was created first Marquis in 1641, played a conspicuous part in the Covenanters' cause against Charles I, and Castle Campbell itself became a Covenanting stronghold.

In 1645 the royalist leader, James Graham, Marquis of Montrose, made a triumphant progress from Fife to his last, and greatest, victory - at Kilsyth - in the course of which he took his army through Dollar. It is recorded that Montrose marched 'waistwards towards Striuelling and in his way he burnes the land of Castell Gloum otherways called Castell Campbell'. The devastating attack on Dollar and Muckhart was apparently carried out by the MacLeans, who had a long-standing feud with the Campbells and seized the opportunity to pay off old scores. The people of Dollar sought parliamentary help to repair the damage and in doing so told of 'whole houses...burnt, their corn destroyed, their bestiall and plenishing taken away...by enemies of this Kirke and kingdome in the rebellioun of James Graham and bloodie Irishes with him'.

James Graham,
Marquis of Montrose.

Some restitution was granted by an Act of Parliament of 1645, by which the timber of the wood of Hairshaw (or Hartshaw), a property of the Stewarts of Rosyth (a royalist then languishing in prison), was awarded to the folk of Dollar and Muckhart. In addition, Argyll was granted 22,000 merks for the relief of the needy. It was long assumed that Castle Campbell was itself destroyed by Montrose. However, while a party of Macleans certainly made a sortie to the walls of the castle and hurled insults at the garrison within, the castle remained in the Covenanters' hands, apparently little damaged. It was only a temporary reprieve, for the end for Castle Campbell came nine years later.

Castle Campbell, Dollar
Glen and the Ochil Hills
from the south.

Argyll's Lodging, Stirling, looking east towards the Ochil Hills and Dollar Glen (left).

Cromwell and the Castle

I n September 1650 Oliver Cromwell's English army defeated the Scots at the Battle of Dunbar. His victory heralded another decade of turmoil for many Scots. Once again, Argyll was at the centre of the action. Having placed the Scottish crown on the head of Charles II at Scone on New Year's Day 1651, he promptly switched loyalty and was party to the proclamation of Cromwell as Lord Protector of Scotland.

Castle Campbell was inevitably caught up in the stirring events that followed. In 1653 Colonel Lilburne, commander-in-chief of the English forces in Scotland, wrote to Cromwell from his base at Dalkeith: 'Hee [Argyll] promises to use his endeavour to his utmost power to preserve peace, and uppon his return from Castle Cammell, which will be shortly, he will send for some of these new engagers, and try if he can convince them of their follie'. Shortly afterwards, the castle was evidently garrisoned by English soldiers, since a requisition for bedding, blankets and such like, dated 26 December 1653, was issued to the burgh of Culross. The castle thus became an obvious target for those objecting to the English occupation.

Archibald Campbell, eighth Earl of Argyll, placing the crown of Scotland on the head of King Charles ll at the coronation held at Scone in 1651 (from a contemporary Dutch broadsheet).

A view west along the hall and chamber range, showing the charred floor boards revealed in the course of excavations in 1982.

The end of the castle as a principal residence of the Argyll Campbells came in 1654. General Monck, writing to Cromwell on 29 July from his base at Stirling, told how 'wee are now come hither where wee shall stay some few days for refreshment. Some small parties of the Enemy are abroad in the country and on Monday and Tuesday nights last burn't Castle Campbell an House belonging to the Marquesse of Argyll'. Graphic evidence of this attack was found during excavations within the hall and chamber range in 1982, when heavily charred floorboards and joists were found on the first floor.

Argyll may have planned to repair the damage when more peaceful times returned but in 1661, the year after Charles II's return to the throne, Argyll was executed for his support of Cromwell's Commonwealth. His son, to whom the earldom but not the marquisate was restored in 1663, preferred to live more spaciously within the burgh of Stirling, where the family had held property for many generations. He acquired what had been the splendid town house of the first Earl of Stirling and further extended it to form the house now known as Argyll's Lodging.

The Campbells abandoned their old castle, but they continued in possession of the lands. As before, they held them from the Bishops of Dunkeld, until the abolition of the office of bishop in the established Church 1698, after which they were held directly from the Crown. It is also clear that the castle could be garrisoned if the need arose, and in the Jacobite rising of 1715 the second Duke placed a small force here. Eventually, having no further use for them, in 1805 the lands were sold by the sixth Duke to Mr Crawford Tait, the owner of the nearby Harviestoun estate, thereby bringing to an end Clan Campbell's long connection with the castle that still bears their name.

The Castle in the Glen

Although Castle Campbell's days as a fortified residence ended in 1654, during the eighteenth and nineteenth centuries the rugged ruins on their dramatic hillside setting above Dollar Glen came to be increasingly appreciated for their picturesque beauty, and many romantic images were made of it. In 1874-5 Sir James Orr of Harviestoun carried out some archaeological investigations of the ruins and took measures to prevent further decay, though the *Alloa Advertiser* of 16 October 1880 could still report that parts of the castle were in a tumbledown condition.

A Ministry of Works (MOW) skew-put on the tower-house roof.

In 1948 Mr Kerr of Harviestoun offered the castle and glen to the National Trust for Scotland, and an agreement was reached whereby the Trust would maintain the glen while the Ministry of Works (the predecessor of Historic Scotland) would care for the castle. Since then the ruins of the castle have been stabilised, a new roof, following the likely form of the original, has been placed on the tower house, and a flat for the steward created in the east range.

The tower house as depicted c. 1840 by Robert Billings, and showing the structure before the present roof was put on.

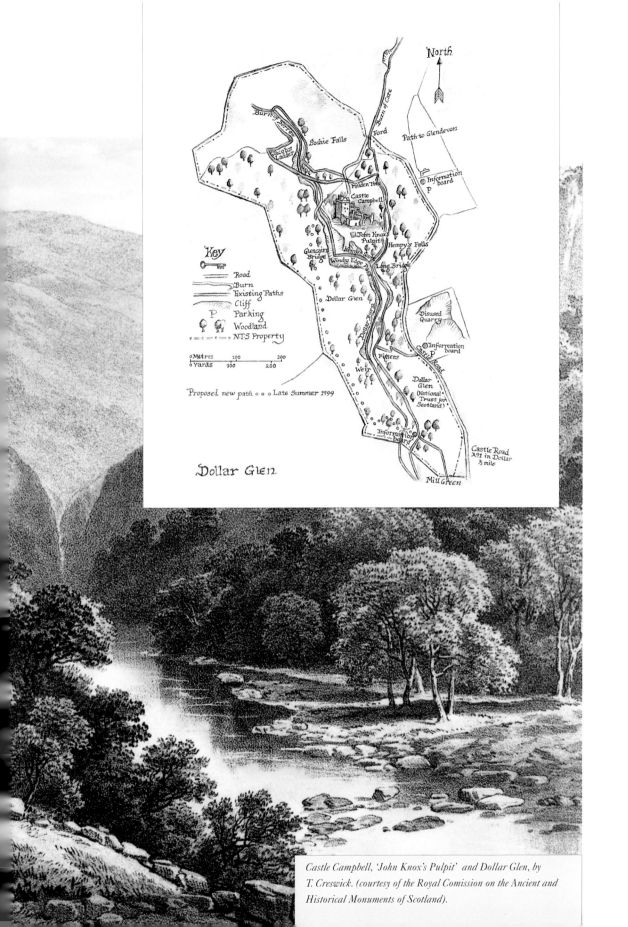

Dollar Glen

Key

- Road
- Burn
- Existing Paths
- Cliff
- P Parking
- Woodland
- NTS Property

Proposed new path o o o Late Summer 1999

North

Burn of Sorrow
Burn of Care
Sochie Falls
Ford
Path to Glendevon
Jacobs Ladder
Information board P
Maiden Tree
Castle Campbell
John Knox's Pulpit
Glencairn Bridge
Hempy's Falls
Kemp's Score
Windy Edge Pass
Long Bridge
Dollar Glen
Disused Quarry
Dollar Burn
Information board P
Fitters
Castle Road
Weir
Dollar Glen (National Trust for Scotland)
Information board
Castle Road A91 in Dollar ½ mile
Mill Green

Metres 0 100 200
Yards 0 100 200

*Castle Campbell, 'John Knox's Pulpit' and Dollar Glen, by
T. Creswick. (courtesy of the Royal Comission on the Ancient and
Historical Monuments of Scotland).*

FURTHER READING

On Castle Campbell:

D MacGibbon and T Ross
*The Castellated and Domestic
Architecture of Scotland*, I (1887)

On the Campbells and their castles:

R Fawcett
Argyll's Lodging, Stirling (1996)

G Harvey Johnston
The Heraldry of the Campbells (1977)

I Lindsay & M Cosh
Inveraray and the Dukes of Argyll (1973)

Royal Commission on the Ancient and
Historical Monuments of Scotland
Inventory of Argyll, vols 2 (*Lorn*, 1975);
3 (*Mull*, 1980); 7 (*Mid Argyll and
Cowal*, 1992)

On castles generally:

S Cruden
The Scottish Castle (1981)

C Tabraham
Scotland's Castles (1997)